Weird America!

America's Oddest Crimes

By Janey Levy

Gareth Stevens Publishing

Please visit our website, www.garethstevens.com. For a free color catalog of all our high-quality books, call toll free 1-800-542-2595 or fax 1-877-542-2596.

Cataloging-in-Publication Data

Names: Levy, Janey.
Title: America's oddest crimes / Janey Levy.
Description: New York : Gareth Stevens Publishing, 2017. | Series: Weird America | Includes index.
Identifiers: ISBN 9781482457438 (pbk.) | ISBN 9781482457452 (library bound) | ISBN 9781482457445 (6 pack)
Subjects: LCSH: Crime–Juvenile literature. | Criminal investigation–Juvenile literature.
Classification: LCC HV6789.L49 2017 | DDC 364.152'3–dc23

First Edition

Published in 2017 by
Gareth Stevens Publishing
111 East 14th Street, Suite 349
New York, NY 10003

Designer: Sarah Liddell
Editor: Ryan Nagelhout

Photo credits: Cover, p. 1 (arrow) Mascha Tace/Shutterstock.com; cover, p. 1 (main) Photographee.eu/Shutterstock.com; cover, p. 1 (banana) Flipser/Shutterstock.com; sidebar used throughout zayats-and-zayats/Shutterstock.com; brick background texture used throughout multipear/Shutterstock.com; screen background texture used throughout donatas1205/Shutterstock.com; p. 5 (main) Image Source/Getty Images; p. 5 (check) Z. Ayse Kiyas Aslanturk/Shutterstock.com; p. 6 Ilaszlo/Shutterstock.com; p. 7 Oscar C. Williams/Shutterstock.com; p. 8 (sponges) TrotzOlga/Shutterstock.com; p. 8 (tuna cans) Kitch Bain/Shutterstock.com; p. 8 (mustard) Warren Price Photography/Shutterstock.com; p. 9 Ampyang/Shutterstock.com; p. 11 New York Daily News Archive/Contributor/New York Daily News/Getty Images; p. 12 (cardboard gun) file404/Shutterstock.com; p. 12 (potato chip bag) Lana Langlois/Shutterstock.com; p. 13 Photographee.eu/Shutterstock.com; p. 14 (camera)NinaM/Shutterstock.com; p. 14 (job application) rCarner/Shutterstock.com; p. 14 (money) Ambient Ideas/Shutterstock.com; p. 15 @mr.jerry/Getty Images; p. 16 Lydia Vero/Shutterstock.com; p. 17 Image Source/Getty Images; p. 18 Roman Samborskyi/Shutterstock.com; p. 19 Iriana Shiyan/Shutterstock.com; p. 20 Maya Morenko/Shutterstock.com; p. 21 eakkaluktemwanich/Shutterstock.com; p. 23 CDA/Wikimedia Commons; pp. 24, 25 Leemage/Getty Images; p. 26 Time Life Pictures/The LIFE Picture Collection/Getty Images; p. 27 Bettman/Contributor/Bettman/Getty Images; p. 28 Eric Isselee/Shutterstock.com; p. 29 (frames) Sabelskaya/Shutterstock.com; p. 29 (tacos) Bochkarev Photography/Shutterstock.com; p. 29 (horse-drawn carriage) David Kay/Shutterstock.com; p. 29 (shrimp) AN NGUYEN/Shutterstock.com; p. 29 (snowman) Anne Kitzman/Shutterstock.com; p. 29 (underpants) PeJo/Shutterstock.com; p. 29 (ouija board) nutech21/Shutterstock.com.

Printed in the United States of America

CPSIA compliance information: Batch #CW17GS: For further information contact Gareth Stevens, New York, New York at 1-800-542-2595.

CONTENTS

Words in the glossary appear in **bold** type the first time they are used in the text.

IT'S A CRIME

Everyone is familiar with the idea of crimes. Our society has laws meant to protect us. A crime happens when you break a law. Some crimes are small. For example, if you park your car illegally, you'll get a parking ticket. Speeding, or driving too fast, is a more serious crime because someone could be hurt. **Robbery** is an even more serious crime. And murder is extremely serious.

Some crimes, however, are just plain weird. They're not meant to be weird—they just turn out that way. And occasionally someone commits a crime accidentally, like the man who laughed too loudly. Keep reading to discover some truly odd crimes!

Illegal Laughter?

A man who lives in Long Island, New York, received two tickets from police for "**disturbing** the peace." His next-door neighbor had complained that he laughed too loudly! For each ticket, the man could be fined $250 or sent to jail for 15 days.

A man walked into a bank in Texas and tried to cash a check for $360 billion. That's right—$360 BILLION. Not surprisingly, the bank clerks were suspicious and called police. The man was arrested and charged with **forgery.**

I WAS HUNGRY, OFFICER!

For some people, committing a crime such as robbery or **burglary** seems the most reasonable way to get food when they're hungry. In Marked Tree, Arkansas, a man broke into a home, made himself a snack, poured himself a glass of tea, and then went outside to eat. Perhaps the name of the street—Pecan Street—made him start to feel hungry.

The police arrested him and took him to jail. When the local TV news talked to the man, he proclaimed his **innocence**—in spite of the fact he was eating the snack and holding the glass of tea when he was arrested!

There are many easier, less costly—and legal—ways to get a banana than crashing your car into a building!

I Really, Really Need a Banana

Early one morning, a man rammed his car into a gas station to break in. But he didn't steal money or gather up lots of goods to take. No, all he wanted was a banana, which he ate right there. Security cameras at the scene captured pictures of the thief, who hadn't bothered with a mask.

It was after midnight in Manassas, Virginia, and one would-be criminal was hungry. You might think the reasonable thing to do would be to go to the kitchen and fix a snack. But he didn't want to go to all that trouble. Instead, he broke into a room at a local inn—so he could order food to be brought to his room!

However, staff at the inn realized there wasn't supposed to be anyone in that room, so they called police. Police came, arrested the man, and charged him with unlawful entry. He probably wished he had just fixed a snack at home!

Party Plans?

One burglar of a Brooklyn, New York, home took numerous cans of tuna fish and salmon, boxes of crackers, and four jars of fancy mustard called Grey Poupon. He also took three bottles of soap, three packages of sponges, and other items. It looked like the robber was stealing to get ready for some sort of party!

The next time you order room service in a hotel, make sure you're in the right room!

ROBBERY GONE WRONG

Bank robbery is a common crime—for reasons that are clear. Most robbers try to hide their **identity** by covering their face with a mask. But one pair of robbers had a better idea. They would be **invisible**! How would they accomplish that? They had a plan based on invisible writing with lemon juice.

You might know how this works: you write in lemon juice, which is invisible on paper. After the lemon juice dries, hold the paper near a heat source, and the writing appears. The bank robbers rubbed lemon juice on their faces to become invisible. Of course, it didn't work, and they were caught and sent to prison!

Robbery as an Escape Plan

This bank robbery was clearly odd. The man had a gun, but didn't **threaten** anyone. After he got the money, he waited for police. He wanted to be caught to get away from someone: his wife! He didn't know how to leave her and figured jail was his only way out!

When asked why he robbed banks, famous bank robber Willie Sutton replied, "Because that's where the money is."

Willie Sutton

Robbers often use a weapon, but not always. However, they may still want their victim to *think* they have a weapon. Consider the following story.

A Rohnet Park, California, man approached a clerk at the car wash and put down an empty potato chip bag. He told the clerk to fill it with money and said there was a gun in it. But the clerk noticed it was just a piece of cardboard inside and called another clerk over. The man ran away. Considering that his plan included a potato chip bag and a piece of cardboard for a gun, the crime doesn't seem to have been very well thought out!

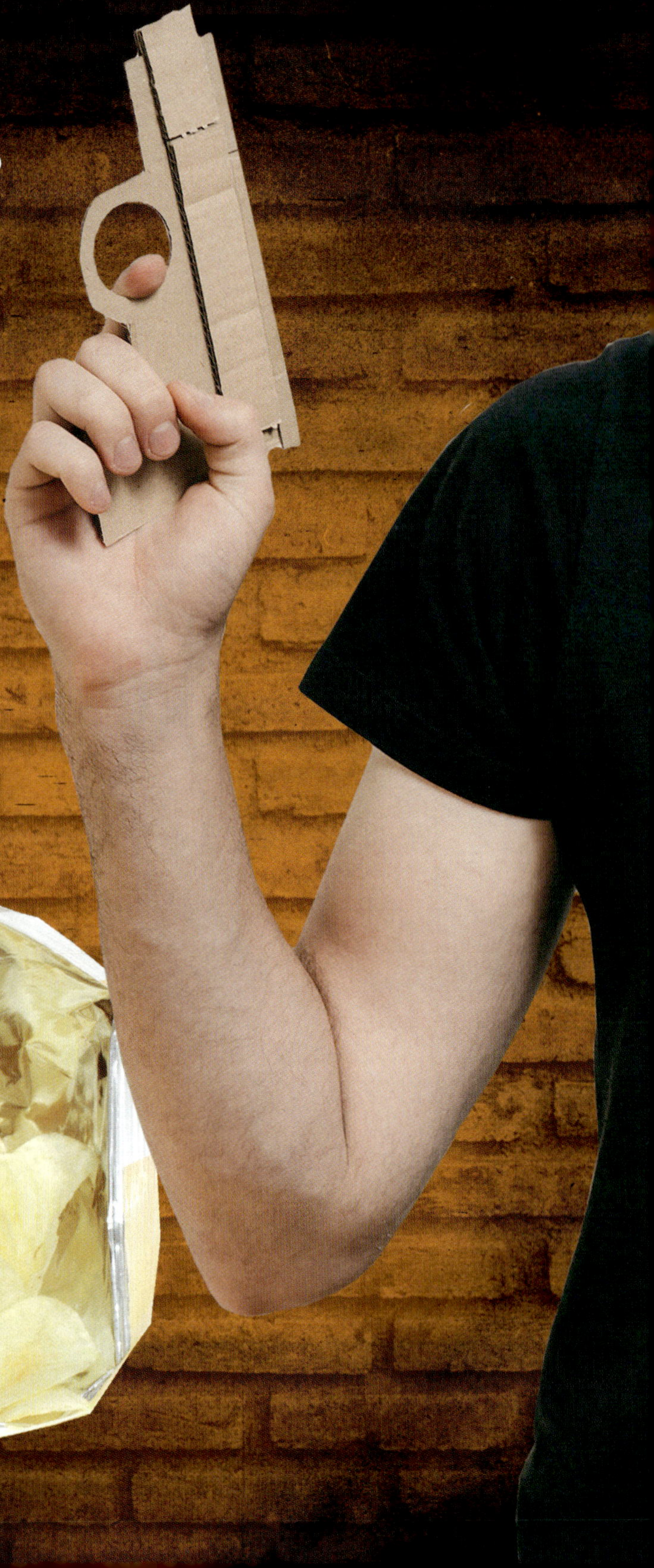

Getting a good night's sleep is important for everyone—even criminals!

Rest Up Before Your Crime

One thief found the effort of stealing everything from a home so tiring that he decided to take a nap. When the homeowner came home and found him asleep, the police were called.

The plan was simple—and perfect. The man would go to a gas station and pretend he wanted to apply for a job. While he was filling out the papers and the clerk wasn't looking, he would grab the money from the cash drawer and run away.

The robbery went just as planned. But police caught the man just a short distance from the gas station. What had gone wrong? Well, the gas station had a security camera, which showed the man stealing the money. And when the man filled out the papers for the job, he used his real name!

Robbing someone trained in **martial arts** like tae kwon do is never a very good idea, especially if the criminal doesn't have a weapon.

Choose Your Victim Carefully

This plan was simple, but far from perfect. The criminal decided to rob a master of tae kwon do (ty kwahn do) in his studio. Tae kwon do is a martial art that places importance on kicking, but the criminal decided he could carry out his robbery without a weapon. The tae kwon do master caught him and held him by the neck until police arrived.

CHEESY CRIMINALS

Well-planned robberies are called heists, and two different heists in 2016 involved lots of cheese. Both crimes also happened in the cheese-crazy state of Wisconsin. In January, a trailer carrying $70,000 worth of cheese was stolen from Germantown, which is near Milwaukee.

Later that year, in July, 20,000 pounds (9,072 kg) of cheese disappeared from a trailer parked in another town near Milwaukee. The driver unhitched the trailer to run an errand. When he returned, the trailer—packed with $46,000 worth of cheese—was gone! The cheese bandits are still on the loose, so watch your cheese if you visit Milwaukee!

You might be surprised to learn that cheese is one of the most commonly stolen items. It's stolen so often that some stores put security tags on it. The tags will set off alarms if the cheese is carried out of the store without being paid for.

More Cheesy Criminals

Two women walked into a grocery store in Bend, Oregon—another state famous for its cheese. They asked the staff in the cheese department to box up some cheese for them. Then the women walked out of the store with $600 worth of cheese—that they hadn't paid for! The women were never caught.

ATTEMPTED MURDER

Murder and attempted murder are serious, even terrible, crimes. But sometimes, people's reasons for committing these crimes are so weird that the whole crime becomes odd. For example, take the case of the man in the story below.

One day, a Utah man began to suffer a severe headache. He became convinced his girlfriend was the cause of his headache. He believed the only way to make the pain go away was to shoot his girlfriend so she would die! The man shot his girlfriend, and neighbors who heard the shot called police. The girlfriend was badly wounded, but fortunately survived. The man was arrested and taken to jail.

What Did You Say?

A man entered a store riding a motorized cart, with his service dog walking beside him. The store manager asked that he please put the dog on a leash. In reply, the man pulled out a gun and shot the manager! The manager survived, and the man was arrested.

A Connecticut man was arrested after an odd bathroom incident. He thought the person inside was taking too long, so he shot at the door!

NOT-SO-DEADLY ASSAULT

Assault with a deadly weapon isn't as serious as murder, but it's still a serious crime. However, one man's choice of weapon made the crime less serious—he attacked his girlfriend with a banana! Since the banana wasn't a deadly weapon, police arrested him for simple assault.

Another food assault happened in 2016, when a Pennsylvania man made dinner for a friend. The friend refused to eat the meal—ramen noodles—and so the man punched his friend in the eye more than a dozen times. The chef was charged with assault and **harassment**.

A Sour Crime

One Milwaukee man was so angry about his late-night taco order he came back to the restaurant to cause trouble. Workers say the man came in angry because they forgot to put sour cream on his order. The man shot at a bulletproof glass window and an employee's car!

Getting hit with a banana would be unpleasant, but at least it wouldn't hurt much!

SOME OF HISTORY'S ODDEST CRIMES

History has its share of weird crimes and odd criminals. George Ebeling, who often worked with William Lowe, has been called the least successful train robber in America. That's certainly not the way he hoped to be known when he started his criminal career.

Ebeling and Lowe's first train robbery took place in 1908. They got $60. That's worth about $1,150 today. And that was one of their most successful train robberies! On their next robbery, they only got $20, or about $385 in today's money. Their third robbery was even worse—$12, or about $230 in today's money. Ouch!

Butch Cassidy and the Sundance Kid

To understand just how bad Ebeling and his partner Lowe were, it helps to compare them to successful train robbers from the period. Perhaps the most famous were Butch Cassidy and the Sundance Kid. When they robbed trains, they got amounts such as $50,000 (or $1,210,000 today), $70,000 ($1,690,000), and $100,000 ($2,420,000)!

Butch Cassidy and the Sundance Kid, pictured here with their gang, were so famous and popular that a movie was made about them in 1969. Ebeling and Lowe would probably have liked to have a movie made about them.

Ebeling and Lowe's last train robbery took place in 1910 near St. Louis, Missouri. They claimed they got over $500 from the robbery, although officials said they stole only $155—about $2,910 in today's money.

Lowe was captured just a few weeks later and named everyone else who took part in the robbery. Ebeling was soon captured, and both men were tried for their crimes. Not surprisingly, they were found guilty. Ebeling spent 15 years in prison. When he got out in 1925, he was 50 years old. Altogether, Ebeling and Lowe had managed to steal just over $1,000 ($18,800). Ebeling's share was $500 ($9,400).

An Odd Ending

While Ebeling was in prison, he met a banker who was there for breaking banking laws. The two men became friends, and the banker promised to give Ebeling a job when he got out of prison. So when Ebeling got out, he looked up his friend and took the job. The train robber went to work in banking!

This French newspaper illustration shows how train robberies looked in the 1900s. Many were more successful than the one Ebeling and Lowe pulled off in 1910.

A more recent odd crime occurred in 1971. On a flight to Seattle, a man calling himself Dan Cooper gave a flight attendant a note saying he had a bomb. He had her take a note to the pilot saying he wanted four **parachutes** and $200,000.

The plane landed in Seattle, he got the parachutes and money, and the plane took off again, headed for Mexico City. On the way, the man jumped from the plane with the money. He did this at night, over a wooded area, using a parachute that couldn't be controlled, wearing clothes that weren't suited for a rough landing. His fate remains a mystery.

artist's sketch of Cooper

D.B. Cooper

The mystery man in this story called himself Dan Cooper, although that's likely not his real name. However, probably as a result of misunderstanding, news stories reported his name as "D.B. Cooper." And to this day, he's still known as D.B. Cooper, and people talk about the D.B. Cooper mystery.

Some of the money Cooper received was discovered in 1980 along the Columbia River by a young boy on a camping trip. Neither Cooper nor the rest of the money has ever been seen.

REALLY WEIRD CRIMES

The weird crimes in this book are just a sampling of the odd things that occur daily across America. For example, a woman tried to use a **coupon** she'd printed from the Internet at a local store. When told the store didn't accept Internet coupons, she threatened people with a gun!

Then there's the guy in Kansas who was caring for a friend's pet spider while the friend was away. When the friend returned and wanted his spider back, the guy said to give him $100 or he'd kill the spider!

Want more weird crimes? Check out the next page!

So Funny It Hurts

Although these crimes can be entertaining to read about, it's important to remember that they *are* crimes. People do get hurt by these criminals. So enjoy the oddness, but don't lose sight of the real harm caused.

MORE CRAZY CRIMES

Taco Bell Terror
A man called the police after a Taco Bell wouldn't sell him tacos while standing in the drive-thru lane.

Horse Hijacking
A Missouri man was arrested for attacking a horse-drawn carriage driver and trying to steal the horse.

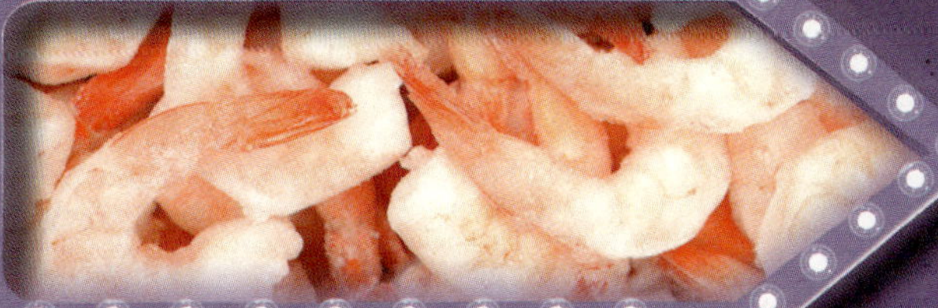

Missing Shrimp
A Florida man tried to attack his stepson with a sword over a missing can of shrimp.

Frosty Killer
Two Ohio teens were arrested after attacking an **inflatable** snowman Christmas decoration with a knife.

Illegal Underwear Prank
A Florida man was arrested for giving wedgies to strangers at a movie theater.

Board Game Murder
A Texas teen blamed a Ouija board for attempted murder.

GLOSSARY

burglary: the crime of breaking into a building for the purpose of stealing

coupon: a piece of paper given to receive some article or some lowering of price of an article

disturb: to destroy the rest of

forgery: the crime of falsely and with the purpose of cheating making or altering a writing

harassment: to worry with repeated physical or verbal attacks

identity: individual existence

inflatable: able to be blown up or swelled with air

innocence: freedom from guilt

invisible: unable to be seen

martial art: any of several arts of fighting and self-defense or protection that are widely practiced as sport

parachute: a specially shaped piece of cloth that collects air to slow something down

robbery: the act or practice of stealing from a person by force or threat of force

threaten: to promise punishment or harm to

FOR MORE INFORMATION

BOOKS

National Geographic. *Weird but True! Stupid Criminals: 150 Brainless Baddies Busted, Plus Wacky Facts.* Washington, DC: National Geographic, 2012.

Wojna, Lisa, and Winter Prosapio. *Weird U.S. Laws: Strange, Bizarre, Wacky & Absurd.* Edmonton, Alberta, Canada: Blue Bike Books, 2012.

WEBSITES

The 10 Weirdest and Wackiest Farm Crimes of 2015
modernfarmer.com/2016/01/farm-crime-2015/
Discover a class of crimes you probably never thought about, and read about some weird ones!

Intruder Begs His Victims for Help and Other Odd Crimes
dailynews.com/article/LA/20131119/NEWS/131119379
Read about more odd crimes from around the country.

Legally Weird
blogs.findlaw.com/legally_weird/strange-crime/
Find more strange crimes on this website for lawyers.

Publisher's note to educators and parents: Our editors have carefully reviewed these websites to ensure that they are suitable for students. Many websites change frequently, however, and we cannot guarantee that a site's future contents will continue to meet our high standards of quality and educational value. Be advised that students should be closely supervised whenever they access the Internet.

INDEX